North American
INDIAN NATIONS

NATIVE PEOPLES
of the
PLAINS

Linda Lowery

LERNER PUBLICATIONS ◆ MINNEAPOLIS

The editors would like to note that we have made every effort to work with consultants from various nations, as well as fact-checkers, to ensure that this content is accurate and appropriate. In addition to this title, we encourage readers to seek out content produced by the nations themselves online and in print.

Content Consultant: Jameson R. Sweet, PhD candidate in History, University of Minnesota; Editorial Manager, Native American and Indigenous Studies

Lerner Publications Company
A division of Lerner Publishing Group, Inc.
241 First Avenue North
Minneapolis, MN 55401 USA

For reading levels and more information, look up this title at www.lernerbooks.com.

Main body text set in Rockwell Std Light 12/16.
Typeface provided by Monotype Typography.

Library of Congress Cataloging-in-Publication Data

Lowery, Linda, 1949–
    Native peoples of the plains / Linda Lowery.
       pages cm. — (North American Indian Nations)
    Includes bibliographical references and index.
    Audience: Grades 4-6.
    ISBN 978-1-4677-7934-0 (lb : alk. paper) — ISBN 978-1-4677-8325-5 (pb : alk. paper) —
ISBN 978-1-4677-8326-2 (eb pdf)
    1. Indians of North America—Great Plains—Juvenile literature. 2. Indians of North
America—Great Plains—History—Juvenile literature. I. Title.
E78.G73L69 2015
978.004'97—dc

232014045363

Manufactured in the United States of America
1 – PC – 7/15/16

CONTENTS

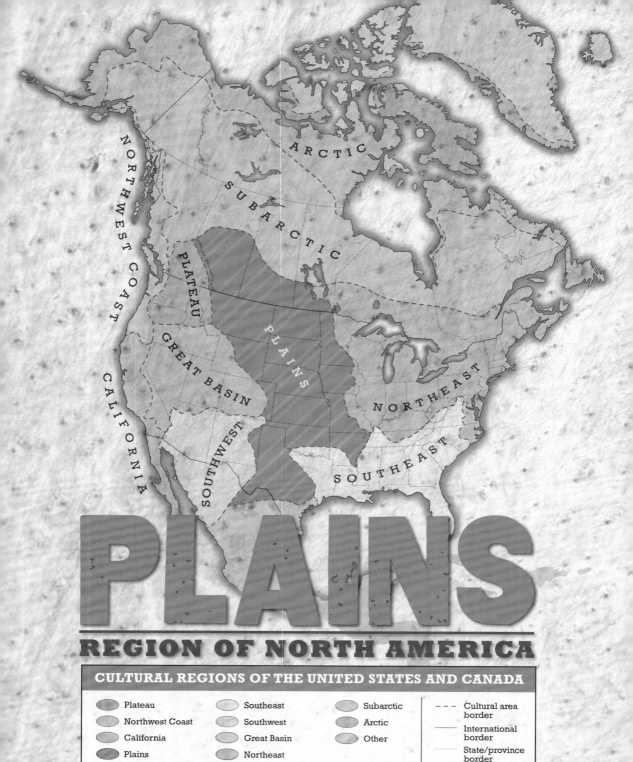

ARCTIC

SUBARCTIC

NORTHWEST COAST

PLATEAU

PLAINS

GREAT BASIN

CALIFORNIA

SOUTHWEST

NORTHEAST

SOUTHEAST

PLAINS
REGION OF NORTH AMERICA

CULTURAL REGIONS OF THE UNITED STATES AND CANADA

- Plateau
- Northwest Coast
- California
- Plains
- Southeast
- Southwest
- Great Basin
- Northeast
- Subarctic
- Arctic
- Other

- – – – Cultural area border
- —— International border
- ········· State/province border

INTRODUCTION

Somewhere on the North American Plains, a campfire glows beneath a bright moon during summer. A group of children sits quietly in a circle. They listen as an elder tells a story. If the children are Arapaho (uh-RA-puh-ho), they may be listening beneath the Moon When the Buffalo Bellow. If the children are Lakota (luh-KO-tuh), they might be under what they call the Moon When the Chokecherries Are Black. To the Comanche (kuh-MAN-chee), it is the Hot Moon.

For thousands of years, native peoples of the plains used the moon to keep track of time. Twelve or thirteen complete phases of the moon made up one year. The Omaha (OH-muh-haw), from present-day Nebraska and Iowa, counted six moons. The Mandan (MAN-dan) and Hidatsa (hih-DAHT-suh)—from modern-day North Dakota and Montana—divided the year into a winter moon and a summer moon.

Plains peoples were the first residents of North America's grassy prairies. Some scholars believe their ancestors came from northeast Asia as early as forty thousand years ago. These people may have traveled by boat or walked across the frozen Bering land bridge that used to stretch between Russia and Alaska. Eventually these first Americans found routes from present-day Alaska to the Great Plains.

PEOPLES OF THE PLAINS

The Plains region is the original home of many American Indian nations. This map shows the areas where some of them lived before Europeans arrived in the region.

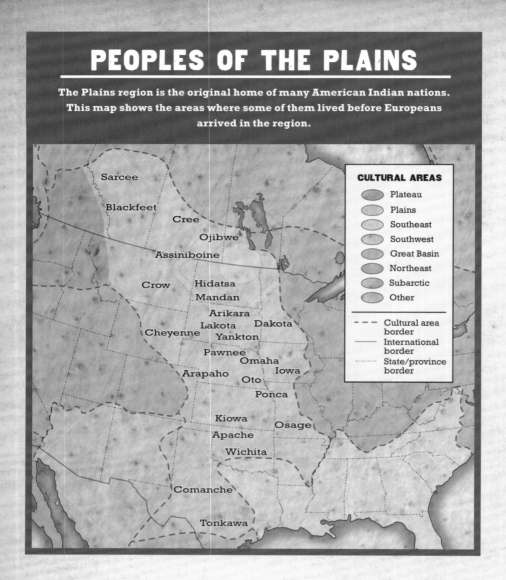

CULTURAL AREAS

- Plateau
- Plains
- Southeast
- Southwest
- Great Basin
- Northeast
- Subarctic
- Other

- – – – Cultural area border
- ——— International border
- ·–·–·– State/province border

Sarcee
Blackfeet
Cree
Ojibwe
Assiniboine
Crow
Hidatsa
Mandan
Arikara
Lakota
Dakota
Cheyenne
Yankton
Pawnee
Omaha
Arapaho
Iowa
Oto
Ponca
Kiowa
Osage
Apache
Wichita
Comanche
Tonkawa

Ancient Plains Indian stories say that Plains peoples have lived in this region much longer—ever since the Great Spirit created Earth. Each Plains culture tells its own version of how this happened. The Pawnee (pah-NEE), of present-day Nebraska and Kansas, say the Morning Star and the Evening Star had a daughter. She was the first human. The Arapaho, from present-day Colorado and Wyoming, say a coyote and a few bison lived on Earth. But there was only one human. He was an old man. He was lonely. With some clay, bison skin, and smoke from his pipe, he made the first people.

The native peoples spread out across the plains between the foothills of the Rocky Mountains all the way east to the Mississippi River. This grassy sweep of land stretches north into Canada and south to the Rio Grande on the present-day US-Mexico border.

Many Nations

The Plains peoples formed many different nations. Each nation had its own form of government, culture, and language. Plains Indians speak languages from seven different language families. A language family includes many different but related languages. Nations in the same language family also share many cultural traits.

Each Plains nation also had its own way of life. The western nations were nomadic. They followed herds of animals that they hunted for meat. For instance, the Comanche moved across the arid plains of Texas and Oklahoma. Farther north, areas in present-day Montana and Wyoming were home to the Crow (KROH). The Cheyenne (shy-ANN) traveled through present-day North Dakota, South Dakota, Montana, and Colorado.

Eastern nations were more settled. They lived near rivers in green areas where they grew crops. The Osage (OH-sage) people farmed in present-day Arkansas and Missouri. The Oto (OH-toh) settled in today's Oklahoma, Missouri, and Iowa. The Kaw (KAH) lived in present-day Kansas, the Kiowa (KY-uh-wuh) were in present-day Oklahoma, and the Ponca (PONG-kuh) lived in present-day Nebraska.

LANGUAGE FAMILIES OF PLAINS PEOPLES

LANGUAGE FAMILY	MAJOR PEOPLES
Algonquian	Arapaho, Blackfeet, Cheyenne, Plains Ojibwe (oh-JIB-way), Plains Cree (KREE)
Athabaskan	Lipan Apache (uh-PAH-chee), Sarcee (SAR-see)
Caddoan	Arikara (uh-RY-kuh-ruh), Caddo (KAH-doh), Pawnee, Wichita (WIH-chuh-tuh),
Kiowan	Kiowa
Siouan	Assiniboine (uh-SIH-nih-BOYN), Crow, Dakota, Hidatsa, Iowa (EYE-uh-wuh), Lakota, Mandan, Missouria (muh-ZUR-ee-uh), Kaw, Omaha, Osage, Oto, Ponca, Yankton
Uto-Aztecan	Comanche
Tonkawa	Tonkawa (TONG-kuh-wuh)

Many nations, such as the Lakota in present-day Iowa and the Dakotas, both farmed and hunted. They were seminomadic. Mostly in winter, they moved around to hunt animals. At other times, they stayed in one place to grow crops.

Changes and Challenges

By the time Spanish explorers first saw the plains in the sixteenth century, about one million American Indians lived on that land. About twenty-eight nations called the Plains region home. Each nation was made up of independent bands. The bands lived separately in their own villages or camps. They had separate hunting grounds. But the whole nation came together for important occasions.

Europeans began moving to the plains in the eighteenth and nineteenth centuries. Plains peoples' lives suddenly changed. Yet the Plains peoples would survive. Many American Indians still live across the plains.

CHAPTER 1

GIFTS OF
THE PLAINS

The Great Plains are vast. Plains peoples called
mountains, prairies, and canyons home. Each nation's
lifestyle depended on where the people lived. The eastern plains
were green, with tall grasses and rich river valleys. These areas
include the eastern parts of what became Oklahoma, Nebraska,
and Kansas and most of modern Missouri, Iowa, and Arkansas.
Most eastern Plains nations, including the Osage, Oto, and
Ponca, farmed. They mostly planted corn, beans, and squash. So
they had fresh food to eat during the harvest, and there was often
plenty of extra food to store for the winter. Along the streams and
lakes, they hunted for quail, turkey, rabbits, elk, and deer.

To the west, the plains grew drier. The prairie grasses were
shorter, and there were fewer rivers and lakes. Most Lakota,
Dakota, Mandan, and Hidatsa lived in the central part of the
western plains. This area includes parts of western Oklahoma
and most of Nebraska, Kansas, Texas, North Dakota, and
South Dakota.

The Cheyenne and Arapaho lived farther west, near the
short grasses at the foot of the Rocky Mountains. Bighorn sheep,

moose, and antelope roamed the land. In summer, people ate dark red chokecherries, dandelion leaves, and prairie turnips that the Lakota called *timpsula*. In autumn, tribes such as the Arapaho gathered sunflower seeds for food.

The Blackfeet (BLACK-feet) lived in the northwestern plains, in what became Montana and parts of Idaho, Wyoming, and Colorado. Winters brought deep snow and freezing winds.

The southern plains, in present-day Oklahoma and Texas, were hot, rocky, and dry. Caves offered shelter for some peoples, including the Kiowa.

Food Sources

For food, Plains Indians gathered wild chilies, cactus, honey, mesquite beans, acorns, pecans, plums, grapes, and prickly pear fruit. Meat sources included rabbits, deer, elk, prairie dogs, and snakes. Most important, herds of bison roamed the plains. They were most common in the dry western plains.

THE SEVEN COUNCIL FIRES

Non-American Indians often use the name Sioux to talk about the Lakota, the Yankton (YANK-tuhn), and the Dakota (duh-KO-tuh). But these native peoples prefer not to use the name Sioux. Instead, they use the name of their nation and band. Several bands exist within each nation. A person from the Hunkpapa band of the Lakota nation is called Hunkpapa Lakota. As a group, the three peoples call themselves the Seven Council Fires. Seven nations make up this group.

Men and boys hunted the bison. Then Plains Indians used every part of the animal. People made dozens of items from one bison. Horns were made into cups, spoons, and rattles. Bones were made into arrowheads and knives. Bison hair was used as padding and made into ropes. The stomach was made into a pouch to carry water and other items. Even the bison droppings were used. There were few trees on the plains for burning, so dried bison chips made handy fuel. Women handled all these tasks. Young girls learned by helping their mothers and grandmothers.

In Plains cultures, women did the farming, cooking, and most of the food gathering. One special food for most Plains peoples was pemmican. Women hung slices of bison outside to dry. Next, they pounded the meat into powder and mixed it with bison fat or bone marrow. Then they added berries and seeds and cut

A herd of bison grazes on prairie grass in western South Dakota. Plains peoples relied heavily on bison for everything from food and clothing to tools and fuel. In modern times, some Plains peoples still raise bison and sell them to earn money.

the mixture into strips. This hearty food lasted for years, so travelers took it along on their journeys.

Homes

People of the plains lived in three main types of homes: earth lodges, grass lodges, and tipis. Most nations, especially in the east, built permanent homes, plus separate, temporary hunting homes. For instance, the Pawnee and the Omaha were farmers. But they went on bison

Some pemmican ingredients—dried bison meat, fruit, and nuts—are displayed next to finished pemmican patties. Plains women used stone tools such as this mortar and pestle to grind and pound the meat into powder.

hunts twice a year. Then they returned home to their villages to plant and harvest their crops. They built sturdy earth lodges at home and used tipis when they traveled.

The majority of Plains Indians lived in tipis, at least for part of the year. A tipi was a cone-shaped structure made of tall wooden poles and covered with bison skin. Inside, people could cook over a fire. Smoke poured out of a hole in the top. Usually, one family lived in each tipi. Tipis made it easy for nomadic American Indians to take down their homes and travel from place to place. Women owned and managed the tipis. Working together, they could take a tipi down in five minutes.

This tipi is on display at the Ulm Pishkun State Park in Montana. During summer months when Plains peoples were on the move in search of food, these portable homes were ideal.

The Hidatsa and Mandan built sturdy round homes out of packed earth. Often part of the home was underground. These homes were so roomy that sometimes forty people, plus a few animals, could fit inside. The Osage built oblong homes out of packed earth. Several families lived together in a lodge.

Other nations, such as the Wichita, lived in grass lodges. They bent big wooden poles into a dome. Then they covered the dome with thatched prairie grass. From the outside, the homes looked like giant haystacks.

Trade and Communication

When people traveled, they often met and traded with members of other nations. The Mandan and Hidatsa ran busy trade centers. Their villages were along the Missouri River in present-day North Dakota. Members of other nations could easily travel by water to reach these villages. Osage from the eastern plains, Comanche from the southern plains, Arapaho from the western plains, and many others came to trade with the Mandan and the Hidatsa.

Traders exchanged animal skins, furs, bison meat, and crops. After Europeans arrived in the region, Plains peoples traded with them too. Plains Indians received guns, axes, kettles, knives, beads, or European clothing in exchange for furs.

To trade with one another, members of many different nations developed a sign language. If they wanted to say "peace," they clasped both hands together. The left hand was down, and the right hand was placed in the palm of the left. There were more than three thousand signs. Each had a different meaning.

Smoke signals were another form of communication. The plains are

European American frontiersmen of the eighteenth century might have carried knives and flint pouches, like the ones included among these items. Plains traders would exchange meat, furs, and other goods for the knives and pouches.

Left: Smoke signals provided a way to communicate across long distances on the flat plains. *Right:* Colorful beads and porcupine quills decorate these leggings made from antelope hide. They may have been worn by a Blackfoot warrior. The bead-and-quill stripes were made with a technique not familiar to the Blackfoot, so they may have gotten the leggings in a trade with another tribe.

flat, so people could see a smoke signal for miles. They sent messages by changing the puffs of smoke from short to long. Some messages warned a friendly band of danger. Others were practical messages that said it was time for dinner.

Clothing

Members of Plains nations wore similar clothing. People used as much material from animals as they could, including the hides, fur, teeth, feathers, and horns. Most men wore deerskin shirts, leggings, and moccasins. Most women wore buckskin dresses and moccasins. They added leggings in cold weather. In winter, people kept warm with cloaks made from bison hide. They lined their moccasins with soft fur from rabbits or bison. In the northern plains, American Indians made snowshoes out of wood to move over snow in winter.

Men from eastern nations, such as the Omaha and Ponca, wore leather caps made of eagle skin. Men from western Plains nations more commonly wore feather headdresses. Kiowa men in Oklahoma also wore turbans made of otter fur.

Members of each nation made these basic forms of clothing differently, depending on their environment and their traditions. But for all Plains Indians, clothing was important for comfort and protection in their daily lives.

CHAPTER 2

SOCIETY AND
SPIRITUALITY

American Indians of the plains believed in a supreme being. People communicated with the spirit world through dreams, visions, music, and dance. The Great Spirit taught that all things on Earth deserve respect. Animals, birds, trees, water, and rocks must be taken care of. Plains peoples believed that all creatures had souls. When hunters killed bison, they always offered prayers and gifts. This was a way to thank the animal for giving its life.

Family Life

The family was at the center of Plains peoples' lives. The family consisted of parents, children, and grandparents. Babies had cradleboards so their mothers could carry them on their backs. Children learned skills and beliefs by watching, listening to, and copying adults around them. Adults taught children the key values of honesty and respect. No child was allowed to interrupt when someone was speaking.

Men and women were respected equally, but they had different responsibilities. The men hunted and led councils.

They also made shields, tools, and weapons. Boys were taught to become brave warriors. Girls learned other skills that were important for their communities' survival and well-being. Women built tipis, butchered bison, farmed, gathered, cooked and preserved food, and made clothing.

Leadership

Each nation had one or more main leaders, called chiefs. Elders were also important leaders. The two groups often met in council. Either the council or all members of the nation could

SUPREME BEINGS OF PLAINS PEOPLES

PEOPLES	SUPREME BEING	NAME MEANING
Lakota, Yankton, and Dakota	Wakan Tanka	The great mystery
Blackfeet	Napi	Old man
Crow	Akbatekdia	He who does everything
Cheyenne	Heammawihio	The wise one above
Osage	Wakonda	The great creator

elect a main chief. The council also made important decisions about the nation and settled disputes among the bands. Sometimes, a council organized war parties. Elders and chiefs planned how to defend themselves against nearby enemies or how to raid an enemy nation to steal food or weapons.

Healers, often called medicine men and medicine women, were honored spiritual leaders. They used prayer and natural medicines to heal the sick and injured. Lakota medicine men had a different spiritual song to go with every type of medicine they used. Healers often inherited their roles. Skills were passed down through families. In many cultures, healers also received knowledge from dreams. Before Europeans came to the plains, some healers from the Lakota and other nations dreamed of changes. They saw visions of people dying and of their lands being taken away. These stories warned people to be careful when white visitors came.

A Crow warrior may have worn an ornament such as this to protect himself in battle. Ornaments were made with sacred objects—in this case, a bear claw. The objects were believed to protect the wearer.

Celebrations

Bands from the same nation gathered once or twice a year. Sometimes it was for a sacred ceremony to honor and celebrate the Great Spirit.

CEREMONIAL PIPES

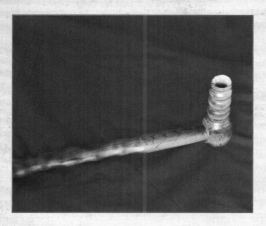

This Shawnee pipe is made of wood. Many other Plains pipes are made of catlinite, a type of soft red stone.

Ceremonial pipes were an important part of life on the plains. The pipes were sacred objects. They were often elaborately decorated. Only men smoked pipes. A group of men passed a pipe in a circle as they prayed. The men prayed for peace or for victory in war. They prayed for help with any decision that would affect the whole nation. Powerful ceremonial pipes have been passed down within nations and treasured for centuries.

Such ceremonies are still common today. Plains peoples often burn a dried long grass called sweetgrass during prayer and healing ceremonies. The smoke is believed to purify people's bodies and spirits. The most important Plains ceremony is the Sun Dance. This is a four-day ceremony asking the Great Spirit to protect the whole community. Many Plains nations, including the Lakota, celebrate the Sun Dance each summer.

During band gatherings, old friends and distant relatives traditionally reunited. Wearing ceremonial clothes, dancing, singing, and playing music are common. This was also customarily a time for families to arrange marriages.

Other times, bands gathered for group bison hunts. Before the hunt began, a medicine man consulted with the Great Spirit. He would ask where the herds were running. When the answer came, the men headed out. Some American Indians, including Lakota men, wore wolf or deer fur over their heads and bodies to sneak up on a herd. Hunters often surrounded bison and shot them with arrows. Several groups, including the Blackfeet, hunted with a technique called the bison jump. Men herded the bison to a cliff, drove them over the edge to their deaths, and collected the bodies below.

Bison are enormous. Adults can weigh 2,000 pounds (907 kilograms). They were far too big for the hunters to drag back to their temporary hunting camp. Instead, the men sent a message

In this painting by European American artist George Catlin (1796–1872), Ojibwe dancers perform a Snowshoe Dance to thank the Great Spirit for the first snowfall.

This cliff, known as Head-Smashed-In Buffalo Jump, in Alberta, Canada, is a UNESCO World Heritage site. Plains hunters would drive bison over cliffs like these.

to the camp. The women traveled with the children, dogs, and tools to meet the men. The women skinned the bison and cut up the meat. They made bags out of the bison skins to carry the meat back to camp. Everyone celebrated with a joyous feast. Bison hunts and the celebrations that followed were key parts of Plains cultures.

CHAPTER 3

ART, MUSIC, AND DANCE

Plains peoples valued artistic skill. Art, music, and dance expressed a deep spiritual connection to plants, animals, and Earth. Art could also record important events.

Pictures and symbols helped Plains peoples stay connected to the Great Spirit. Every pattern and symbol had a special meaning. To the Lakota, three diamonds painted in a row might represent the Wakan Tanka, who watches over humans from above. To the Blackfeet and other nations, a picture of the Morning Star meant power and protection.

Plains Indians also painted small figures and symbols on bison hide, tipis, horses, and clothing. Pictures told stories of battles, the Great Spirit, bison herds, and daily life. The winter count is a special type of picture art. Each year, one picture is added to a piece of hide. That picture tells the story of the most important community event that happened during that year. The Blackfeet, Mandan, Kiowa, and many other Plains nations kept a winter count.

To make the paint for the pictures, Plains peoples used berries, wildflowers, roots, and rocks. They pounded minerals

Lakota winter count keeper Lone Dog created this winter count between the years of 1801 and 1876. Each year, a new event is added to the winter count. A council of elders helps choose the event to be painted each year, and the community's keeper adds the symbol.

and clay into powder and then added bison fat to make a paste. Different plants could create a wide range of colors. The Blackfeet especially valued the color red. They made six different tones of red from the minerals in the northern mountains and rivers.

Before battle, warriors painted symbols on their shirts, shields, weapons, and faces. A Dakota warrior painted his face black. Then, using his fingernail, he scraped a zigzag line from his forehead down to his chin. Mandan warriors painted their bodies reddish brown. Then they drew powerful symbols in red or black on their arms.

Decorative Items

Each nation had a distinctive way of sewing or decorating clothing. People from one nation could identify members of other nations by their clothes. For instance, Kiowa women painted yellow and green designs on their long deerskin dresses. The Comanche, Apache, Pawnee, and Kiowa hung twisted leather fringe on their clothes and bags. Eastern Plains Indians often sewed peacock feathers on their clothes. Most western Plains women—especially from Crow, Blackfeet, Cheyenne, and Arapaho nations—sewed elk teeth, animal hair fringe, and feathers onto clothing. They used hollow porcupine quills as beads. Once trading with Europeans began, many nations added small metal cones, pieces of silver, and mirrors to their clothes. Northern Plains Indians, including the Mandan, Lakota, Dakota, and Cheyenne, are famous for their elaborate beadwork.

A beaded bison hide dress from South Dakota

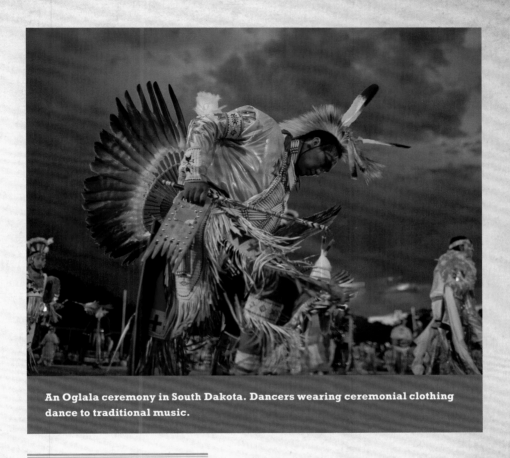

An Oglala ceremony in South Dakota. Dancers wearing ceremonial clothing dance to traditional music.

Music and Dance

To honor the Great Spirit, Plains Indians played music and danced. This was a way of praying. A sacred ceremony began with rattles and drums. The sound of the drums represented the beating of a heart. Then singers joined in. They sang songs of thanks for the seasons. They asked their ancestors to watch over them. They sang to heal the sick, to pray for rain, or to ask for a good bison hunt. The dancers moved to the music in a circle. Their feet stomped to echo the beat of animal hooves.

CEREMONIAL DANCES OF PLAINS PEOPLES

PEOPLES	DANCE	PURPOSE
Caddo	Turkey Dance	To honor the accomplishments of warriors
Kiowa	Gourd Dance	To tell stories of lost warriors
Lakota and Dakota	Ghost Dance	To restore the traditional ways (dance begun in the late 1800s)
Mandan	Bull Dance	To locate bison herds
Omaha and Ponca	Grass Dance	To honor ancestors and gain strength from mother earth

But artistic expression was not always serious. Gatherings called powwows involved social songs and dances. People also played music at smaller social events. Young Plains men, especially among the Lakota, carved flutes to play music to young women they hoped to marry. A young Lakota man would sit wrapped in a blanket and play his flute in front of a young

Left: **A Ponca hand drum decorated with painted symbols.** *Right:* **A hand-carved wooden flute**

woman's tipi. If she came out to join him, it was a promising sign of an engagement to come. Like many other native peoples' traditions, this Lakota custom blended artistic expression with everyday life on the plains.

CHAPTER 4

EUROPEANS
ARRIVE

In 1541, Spanish explorer Francisco Vásquez de Coronado was the first European to come to the Plains region. In present-day Texas and New Mexico, he met the Wichita, Lipan Apache, and Comanche. Other explorers came after him. The explorers and native peoples began trading. The Spanish wanted bison hides, moccasins, and robes. American Indians wanted horses, which are not native to the Americas. Once the Comanche and Apache had horses, these nations brought horses north and east to trade with other nations. By 1700, most Plains nations had horses.

For nearly three hundred years, from the sixteenth century to the nineteenth century, Europeans came to the plains and then usually left. The Cheyenne met and traded with the French in present-day Minnesota. Some Europeans stayed, however. In present-day northern Montana and Canada, white people built trading posts. The Blackfeet brought the pelts of beavers, wolves, and foxes to trade. They exchanged them for ice chisels, axes, blankets, metal knives, mirrors, guns, and glass beads. But the Blackfeet were cautious. They wanted Europeans to visit and to trade with them. But they did not want them to stay permanently. They were fiercely protective of their land.

Treaties Begin

After the American Revolutionary War (1775–1783), a new country took shape along the East Coast: the United States. The US government began making treaties with Plains nations in 1805. These treaties often gave Plains Indian land to the US government. In exchange, American Indian nations were promised a small portion

A beaver pelt is stretched across a hoop of bent sticks. Many American Indian peoples traded furs like this with Europeans in exchange for other valuable goods.

of land set aside for them, money, and other goods. But often the American Indians were threatened or forced to sign treaties against their will. And the US government frequently didn't follow through on the promises they'd agreed to in the treaties.

By the mid-nineteenth century, relations between the government and the Plains Indians became even more strained. Already by this point, there had been many cases of violence against the Plains peoples by the US government. And the eastern United States was becoming an increasingly expensive place to live. Europeans wanted to move west, where land was cheaper. The US government wanted even more for American Indians to give up their land. The United States pressured Plains

FIRST ENCOUNTERS BETWEEN PLAINS INDIAN PEOPLES AND EUROPEANS

YEAR	PLAINS PEOPLES	EUROPEANS
1541	Apache	Spanish explorer Juan de Oñate
1601	Wichita	Spanish explorer Francisco Vásquez de Coronado
1680	Cheyenne	French explorer Sieur de La Salle
1720	Pawnee and Oto	Spanish soldier Pedro de Villasur
1738	Mandan	French fur trader Sieur de La Vérendrye

nations to make more treaties. In 1851, ten thousand Plains Indians, including Arapaho, Cheyenne, and Lakota, signed a treaty at Horse Creek in present-day Wyoming. They agreed to move away from white settlements. In return, US pioneers said they would stay out of areas assigned to American Indians.

Then, in 1859, gold was discovered in Colorado. Thousands of white Americans headed west, hoping to get rich. These people poured into Arapaho and Cheyenne territory and built settlements right beside American Indian villages.

Relations were strained between the two groups. Soon US soldiers forced Cheyenne and Arapaho people off their land. American Indians struck back, sometimes killing pioneers. To keep the peace, the US military built forts on traditional Arapaho and Cheyenne hunting lands.

Removal to the West

After the Civil War (1861–1865), the US government formed a plan to move Plains Indians to reservations. Government officials knew the bison was the western Plains Indians' most valuable source of food, shelter, and clothing. The government encouraged white newcomers to kill bison for sport. The size of bison herds decreased rapidly. This weakened many western Plains nations, including the Lakota, Dakota, Kiowa, and Apache.

General William T. Sherman *(third from left, facing the camera)* meets with American Indian leaders at Fort Laramie, Wyoming, in 1868. The peace treaty signed that day set aside land in the Black Hills of South Dakota for peoples of the Lakota, Dakota, and Arapaho nations.

In exchange for food, blankets, and clothes, Plains nations signed more and more of their land away in treaties.

Plains Indians were also battling illnesses. Europeans carried diseases that were new to the plains. These contagious diseases, such as measles and whooping cough, killed thousands of Plains Indians. Four thousand Comanche died of smallpox. The Blackfeet, Pawnee, Dakota, and other northern nations each lost about one-third of their people to disease. In one Mandan village of sixteen hundred people, only thirty-one survived.

The US government signed many more treaties with Plains nations in 1871. But in 1874, gold was discovered in the Black Hills. The United States ignored one of its treaties with the native peoples in these areas. Europeans rushed to find their fortunes on the land that had been set aside for the Lakota in present-day South Dakota.

Growing Conflict

By the mid-1870s, the US government and the western Plains Indians were at war. The US government had refused to honor treaties to stay off nation lands in the Black Hills. In 1876, a major battle took place. Lakota chief Sitting Bull led the Lakota, Cheyenne, and Arapaho against the US Army, led by General George Custer. The American Indian forces won the Battle of Little Bighorn. But the US government changed the treaty afterward. The Black Hills would not be part of Lakota reservation property anymore.

By 1889, the US government had forced all Plains Indians onto reservations. Most reservations were located in what became Oklahoma and South Dakota. The Northern Arapaho were moved from present-day Colorado to Wyoming. The Lakota were restricted to a small area of the South Dakota land they originally called home.

This photograph, taken in 1890 by John C. H. Grabill, shows a group of American Indians posing between two tipis on the Cheyenne River Reservation in South Dakota.

Even on reservations, violence continued. In December 1890, soldiers entered a Lakota camp at Wounded Knee Creek on the Lakota reservation. They killed nearly three hundred Lakota people. Many were women, children, and elders.

US Citizens

Beginning in 1860, US government officials pressured American Indian parents to send their children to boarding schools run by Christian missionaries. There, teachers tried to make children follow Christianity instead of their traditional beliefs. The teachers cut the children's hair and made them wear uniforms. The children were forbidden to speak their native languages. Many Plains Indians resisted these changes.

At the same time they were speaking out against injustices, some American Indians also helped the US government by serving in the military. Many American Indians fought as soldiers in World War 1 (1914–1918). Because they were US soldiers, they were given US citizenship.

Most other American Indians became US citizens in 1924, when the Indian Citizenship Act became law. The government also made other changes in its policies toward American Indians. The Indian Reorganization Act of 1934, for example, allowed American Indian nations to create their own governments on reservations. These governments had to be based on the US system of government, not on the nations' traditional forms of leadership, however.

By the 1950s, the US government decided to close down many reservations to save money. The government's new plan was to bring American Indians into cities. US leaders hoped that American Indians would give up their cultural identities and blend in with other Americans. Later, the Indian Relocation Act of 1956 encouraged more American Indians to move off reservations and train for jobs in major cities. These plans did not work. Many people had trouble finding jobs because of

This photograph shows a group of schoolboys outside of a Dakota Indian mission school in the late nineteenth century.

LAKOTA AND COMANCHE CODE TALKERS

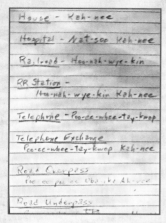

House -	Kah-nee
Hospital -	Nat-soo Kah-nee
Railroad -	Hoo-nah-wye-kin
RR Station -	Hoo-nah-wye-kin Kah-nee
Telephone -	Poo-ee-whee-tay-kwop
Telephone Exchange	Poo-ee-whee-tay-kwop Kah-nee
Road Overpass	tie ee pee ee Oba ike Ah-vee
Road Underpass	

A Comanche codebook

During World War II (1939–1945), several Lakota and Comanche servicemen worked as code talkers. These men used their native languages to send and receive secret messages for the US Army. They did this by using code words in their own languages.

It took a machine up to four hours to transmit and decode a Lakota or Comanche message. A code talker could decode the same message in less than three minutes. The United States' enemies never broke these codes.

discrimination. Others were homesick for their homelands and their families. So Plains Indians often returned to reservations.

During the 1960s and 1970s, Plains Indians began looking for new ways to regain their lands and their rights. Many members of Plains nations joined the American Indian Movement (AIM), an activist organization started in 1968. The group wanted the US government to treat American Indian nations more fairly. It also encouraged American Indians to be proud of their cultures. Plains Indians took part in public protests against the US government's treaty violations. They also restarted and shared old traditions such as the Sun Dance. Through AIM and other groups, Plains peoples worked to reclaim their pasts and shape their futures.

CHAPTER 5

KEEPING TRADITIONS ALIVE

In the twenty-first century, Plains Indians belong to two nations. They are citizens of the United States. They are also citizens of their own nations.

Each nation is a small country. It has its own government, laws, and police. Nation members elect men and women to be council members that handle nation business. Reservations are usually the centers of government.

Plains Indians live all around the world. They are members of their nations no matter where they live. Most return to reservations to visit relatives, attend ceremonies, and vote in their nations' elections.

Preserving Traditions

Nation elders, chiefs, and educators work hard to keep their traditional cultures alive. It is difficult work. For instance, in the early 1990s, the Comanche Nation had fifteen thousand members, but only about one hundred still spoke the language. So Comanche leaders started educational programs on reservations to teach preschool children how to speak and write Comanche. In 1995, the Blackfeet created the Real Speak schools for students in kindergarten through eighth grade. All classes are taught in the Blackfeet language.

Many Plains nations run their own museums. At these museums, visitors can learn about how American Indians of the plains lived in the past. Some Plains activists speak out about the mistreatment of their peoples by Europeans and by the US government. Because of these activists, in 1989, South Dakota changed October 12 from Columbus Day to Native Americans' Day. In 2014, Minneapolis, Minnesota, began to celebrate Indigenous Peoples Day on October 12. It is a day to honor the history and contributions of American Indians.

Facing Challenges

Because it can be hard to find jobs on reservations, most Plains reservations struggle with poverty. Few members can afford to start their own businesses. Some Plains Indians work in casinos owned by their nations. But while these casinos are an important source of employment, they don't provide enough jobs to lift many Plains peoples out of poverty.

Most Plains peoples move to cities for work. Plains peoples have also started their own businesses. Some specialize in green energy, fashion design, jewelry, or construction. Some own restaurants that serve native foods.

Organizations outside reservations also help Plains Indians stay connected to their cultures. In Chicago, Denver, and Minneapolis, people gather at a regional American Indian Center. They join in community meetings, classes, art displays,

In 2014, members of the Oglala Lakota Nation participated in a rally in Pierre, South Dakota, to protest the proposed Keystone XL pipeline.

indigenous food tastings, and powwows. Sometimes elders tell a nation's stories at these centers.

Defending Lands

Plains Indians find many ways to hold onto their values. Sometimes that means resisting outsiders' attempts to use their lands. This happened on the Northern Cheyenne Reservation in Montana. The area is full of green hills and home to wild horses. In the 1960s, coal was discovered underground there. Energy companies wanted to mine the coal. They offered to pay the Cheyenne large sums of money for the land. But to remove the coal, companies had to harm the environment. Mining meant jobs for nation members. But it also meant the land would be destroyed. The Cheyenne voted against coal mining. The coal companies keep making offers, but the Cheyenne continue to turn them down.

In the twentieth century, many Plains nations protested the past unjust treatment by the US government. The Lakota continue to demand the return of their most sacred land—the Black Hills. The government has offered the nation $1.3 billion in place of the land. The Lakota refuse to accept it. They want the land, not the money.

Plains Indians continue to shape history by preserving and teaching about their cultures, values, and traditions. More and more, they share them with non–American Indians. Some display their art. Some play music for big audiences. Some teach their histories and cultures at schools and universities. Many are determined to pass their values on to new generations in their own nations—and across the world.

NOTABLE PLAINS INDIANS

Sarah EchoHawk (Pawnee) is the chief executive officer of the American Indian Science and Engineering Society. This group supports American Indians studying science, technology, engineering, and math. EchoHawk works to help American Indian people build careers in these fields.

Billy Mills (Oglala Lakota) is a track-and-field athlete from South Dakota. He competed in the 1964 Olympics and became the first US athlete to win the 10,000-meter (6.2-mile) run. This also made him the second American Indian to win an Olympic gold medal.

N. Scott Momaday (Kiowa) is a writer of poems, essays, and fiction. He won the 1969 Pulitzer Prize for Fiction for his novel *House Made of Dawn*. His books focus on Kiowa history, customs, and beliefs.

Sean Sherman (Oglala Lakota) is a chef who works in Minnesota. His catering business, The Sioux Chef, serves dishes inspired by traditional Dakota, Lakota, and Ojibwe foods. He uses traditional Plains Indian ingredients, including chokecherries, wild onions, cattails, deer, and bison.

Maria Tallchief (Osage) was a prima ballerina born in 1925 in Oklahoma. She received many honors, including a 1999 National Medal of Arts. She was the first American to perform at the famous Bolshoi Theater in Moscow, Russia.

Timeline

Each Plains Indian culture had its own way of marking time and recording history. This timeline is based on the Gregorian calendar, which Europeans brought to North America.

1541 Spanish explorer Francisco Vásquez de Coronado makes contact with Plains peoples, including Comanche, Wichita, and Lipan Apache.

1805 Plains nations start signing treaties with the US government.

1851 Arapaho, Cheyenne, and Lakota leaders sign the Horse Creek Treaty with the US government.

1859 The Colorado Gold Rush begins, bringing more outsiders to the Plains.

1865 The US government begins forcing Plains Indians onto reservations.

1874 Gold is discovered in the Black Hills, South Dakota. Miners rush in and claim that this land is legally theirs.

1876 The Battle of Little Bighorn is fought between the US government and the Lakota, Cheyenne, and Arapaho.

1890 US soldiers kill nearly three hundred Lakota at the Wounded Knee Massacre.

1917–1918 Plains Indian men fight in World War I and are granted US citizenship.

1924 The Indian Citizenship Act officially grants US citizenship to all American Indians.

1934 The Indian Reorganization Act officially recognizes independent governments of Plains Indian nations.

1941–1945 Lakota and Comanche servicemen become code talkers and play an important role in World War II.

1956 The Indian Relocation Act encourages American Indians to move off reservations.

1968 The American Indian Movement starts. Many members of Plains nations work to make the US government treat American Indians more fairly.

2014 Minneapolis, Minnesota, begins celebrating Indigenous Peoples Day on October 12.

Glossary

band: a group that is part of a larger nation

council: a meeting to discuss important decisions and share advice

cradleboard: a baby carrier with a firm frame lined with soft materials

discrimination: unfair behavior toward others based on differences, such as race, age, or gender

language family: a group of similar languages

missionary: a religious worker who tries to spread his or her religion

nation: a group of people with a shared history, culture, and governing system

nomadic: traveling from place to place rather than settling in one spot

peoples: nations or groups of related nations

powwow: a gathering with traditional dancing, feasting, singing, drumming, and contests

reservation: an area of land set aside by the US government for the use of an American Indian nation

scholar: a person who professionally studies a topic

treaty: a formal written agreement

Selected Bibliography

Freedman, Russell. *Who Was First? Discovering the Americas*. New York: Clarion Books, 2007.

Jennings, Francis. *The Founders of America*. New York: Norton, 1993.

Taylor, Colin F. *The Plains Indians: A Cultural and Historical View of the North American Plains Tribes of the Pre-Reservation Period*. London: Salamander Books, 1994.

Treuer, Anton. *Indian Nations of North America*. Washington, DC: National Geographic, 2010.

Zimmerman, Larry J., and Brian Leigh Molyneaux. *Native North America*. Norman: University of Oklahoma Press, 2000.

Further Information

Capaldi, Gina, and Q. L. Pearce. *Red Bird Sings: The Story of Zitkala-Ša, Native American Author, Musician, and Activist.* Minneapolis: Carolrhoda Books, 2011. Read this story about a Yankton girl who found herself caught between two worlds and shared her gifts with both.

Erdrich, Louise. *The Birchbark House.* New York: Hyperion Books for Children, 1999. This fascinating book tells the story of a young Ojibwe girl named Omakayas who lived on an island in Lake Superior around 1847.

Josephson, Judith Pinkerton. *Who Was Sitting Bull? And Other Questions about the Battle of Little Bighorn.* Minneapolis: Lerner Publications, 2011. Learn more about the Battle of Little Bighorn and how westward expansion of the United States affected Plains Indians.

Kiowa Tribe of Oklahoma
https://www.kiowatribe.org
You will find information on projects and events as well as a Kiowa newsroom at this official site from the Kiowa of Oklahoma.

Mission US: A Cheyenne Odyssey
http://www.mission-us.org/pages/mission-3
Role-play as a twelve-year-old Northern Cheyenne child. Find out how your life changes when soldiers start moving onto your nation's land. You can hear the Cheyenne language spoken too.

Nelson, S. D. *Black Elk's Vision: A Lakota Story.* New York: Abram's Books for Young Readers, 2010. Find out about the life of a famous Lakota medicine man, from the visions he had as a young boy to how he fought at Wounded Knee.

Texas Indians: A Learning and Activity Book
http://www.tpwd.state.tx.us/publications/pwdpubs/media/pwd_bk_p4000_0016.pdf
Print off the pages from this book filled with games and activities. Learn about Texas Plains nations from ancient times to the twenty-first century.

Index

Photo Acknowledgments

The images in this book are used with the permission of: © iStockphoto.com/Bastar (paper background); © lienkie/123RF.com (tanned hide background); © Erick Todd/E+/Getty Images, pp. 2-3; © Laura Westlund/Independent Picture Service, pp. 4, 6; © All Canada Photos/Alamy, p. 12; © Marilyn Angel Wynn/NativeStock/Getty Images, pp. 13, 31; © Danita Delimont/Alamy, p. 14; © Dorling Kindersley/Getty Images, p. 15; © Bettman/Corbis, p. 16 (left); © Werner Forman/Corbis, p. 16 (right); © Bear Claw Medicine/Werner Forman Archive/Bridgeman Images, p. 20; © Marilyn Angel Wynn/Nativestock.com, pp. 21, 26, 29 (top); © MPI/Getty Images, p. 22; © 2003 Wolfgang Kaehler/LightRocket/Getty Images, p. 23; © Corbis, p. 25; © National Geographic Image Collection/Alamy, p. 27; © Nancy G Western Photography/Alamy, p. 29 (bottom); National Archives (111-SC-95986), p. 33; The Granger Collection, New York, p. 35; © Denver Public Library/Western History Collection/Bridgeman Images, p. 36; © Mark Pellegrini/Wikimedia Commons (CC BY-SA 2.5), p. 37; © Andrew Burton/Getty Images, p. 40.

Front cover: © iStockphoto.com/EyeEm.